Litany for the City
by
Ryan Teitman

❖

Winner, 2011 A. Poulin, Jr. Poetry Prize
Selected by Jane Hirshfield

Litany for the City

Poems by

Ryan Teitman

Foreword by Jane Hirshfield

A. POULIN, JR. NEW POETS OF AMERICA SERIES, NO. 34

BOA Editions, Ltd. ❖ Rochester, NY ❖ 2012

First Edition
12 13 14 15   7 6 5 4 3 2 1

For information about permission to reuse any material from this book please contact The
Permissions Company at www.permissionscompany.com or e-mail permdude@eclipse.net.

Publications by BOA Editions, Ltd.—a not-for-profit corporation
under section 501 (c) (3) of the United States Internal Revenue
Code—are made possible with funds from a variety of sources, includ-
ing public funds from the New York State Council on the Arts, a state
agency; the Literature Program of the National Endowment for the
Arts; the County of Monroe, NY; the Lannan Foundation for support
of the Lannan Translations Selection Series; the Mary S. Mulligan
Charitable Trust; the Rochester Area Community Foundation; the
Arts & Cultural Council for Greater Rochester; the Steeple-Jack

ART WORKS.
arts.gov

State of the Arts

NYSCA

Fund; the Ames-Amzalak Memorial Trust in memory of Henry Ames, Semon Amzalak and
Dan Amzalak; and contributions from many individuals nationwide. See Colophon on page
80 for special individual acknowledgments.

Cover Design: Sandy Knight
Interior Design and Composition: Richard Foerster
Manufacturing: Thomson-Shore
BOA Logo: Mirko

Library of Congress Cataloging-in-Publication Data

Teitman, Ryan T.
Litany for the city / by Ryan Teitman. — 1st ed.
    p. cm.
ISBN 978-1-934414-80-4 (pbk. : alk. paper)
I. Title.
PS3620.E437L58 2012
811'.6—dc23

2011036882

BOA Editions, Ltd.
250 North Goodman Street, Suite 306
Rochester, NY 14607
www.boaeditions.org
A. Poulin, Jr., Founder (1938–1996)

For my parents

Contents

FOREWORD

"I want to find the line // where the city becomes the city, / where invention becomes instrument," Ryan Teitman writes, in *Litany for the City*, a first book muscular with transformation. Invention is Ryan Teitman's clay—phrase after phrase coins startling newness out of the things of this world. Watercress, almonds, and oranges; breath, eyelid, sweat; knife, wool, bridge, grease, film, cello, beer cans—daily particulars become in these poems the instruments of a largeness that moves sometimes outward, sometimes within:

> —how a whisper
> between two palms
> becomes an architecture
> we can't fit into
> our mouths. We hear
> words like *nave*
> and remember shoveling
> piles of tulips into
> a burnt-out flatbed.

"I want to find the line // where the city becomes the city, / where invention becomes instrument"— Line matters, too, in this book. The line thrown out to catch a fish, the line of a thought hard-pursued, the map's line-edge that marks where one parcel ends and another begins, the line of music and of music interrupted, the provisional chalk-line a carpenter makes preceding the cut. There is a line that draws the circles of hell, the line of narrative that turns stars to constellations, the line of tactfulness left uncrossed.

Poetry, like architecture, is made by precision of tool and accurate articulation, and Teitman's lines are as variable in their techniques as in their meaning. The sample above reveals the honing stone of his enjambments. A block of prose-poems, "Metropolitan Suite," brings to mind the thinking in Italo Calvino's *Invisible Cities;* conjoining reality's brickwork and imaginative freedoms, each has the depth of field of a stereopticon image, merging inner and outer, possible and created. Other poems stand in narrow columns, step forward in two- or three-line stanzas, walk the full field of the page. The voice here is equally supple—poems take the imperative, offer propositions, remember, tell stories, staccato in fragments. Reading through this book is like walking the blocks of certain aging cities—you never know what might be next: a Hungarian spice and bead store, a glass office tower, a shoe repair shop spilling onto the street the scent of leather, glue, and polish, an anonymous three-story tenement whose upper windows flash a red geranium or flutter with laundry. Each poem is an inhabitance both fully itself and part of a greater whole.

Kinetic prowess leaps from Teitman's descriptions—in one poem, the Delaware river is shown "rippling like a singing saw," in another, a movie's rendered whale bones transform to "a row // of piano keys dipped in honey"; a moment later, we leave the theater to see a burning building whose smoke has infused the whale-film, "its architecture evolving from form to fume." Teitman's images fill the eye, the mouth, the ear; the tongue saying them spills with the pleasure of consonants and vowels set to conscious awareness.

Yet this is a book that holds also much grief, inside its versatile beauties:

> [...] and I want to forget
> when I was five, and our teacher told us to draw
>   a picture of ourselves, and I drew the skyline above the sea,
> said I was changing my name to "The City,"
>   and she leaned in close and said that I would never be
> the city that swallowed the sea, and my face
>   turned warm, and her breath was the dry hush
> of the sea as it slides each day from the city,
>   and we rope and haul it back like a brindle calf
> with three legs tied, and we drink it a little
>   each day, and the censusman knocks every morning
> to measure how much we drank [...]

In such lines, there is enormous imaginative reach, but also the pain of an otherness both its own cause and cure. This book is scented with a recurrence of honey, but also with a recurrent smoke: the heat of renderings, soot, fireworks, charred dismantlings, fevers. What lives here lives in a burning house, lit sometimes by candles, sometimes by pyres: "Morning pulls light / from the dark like a boy / hoisting a trout from the lake / by its clean, pink gills." The image mixes light and dark, death and life, the four elements of air, water, the earth the boy must stand on, the future fire of that fish's cooking for breakfast. This is Ryan Teitman's sustenance: denying no part of what it is to live on this earth. What we eat, dies. Any day is made by labor, starts with the effort of "hoisting." The gills by which one form of oxygen is exchanged for another are beautiful and clean, dawn-pink; they are also the vulnerable edge of opening by which the trout is taken, lifted from one condition of existence into another.

"I want to find the line // where the city becomes the city, / where invention becomes instrument." When I first encountered Ryan Teitman's title, I leaned toward the city in it, and that is, to be sure, an abiding presence. But the more I've read this book through, the more I've come to find its heart is in the *litany*: in the persevering faith that words under pressure can charge and change language to something more than itself, that objects and beings can be liberated into new-parsed comprehensions by their protean, heat-pressured praising. The goal of these pages is not a parcel map of experience, but the enacting of a profoundly instrumental relationship to awareness. And this is a becoming Ryan Teitman has not only wanted to find—he has amply, prodigiously found it.

—Jane Hirshfield

I.

LITANY FOR THE CITY

Philadelphia, 1976

A still night has its own cruel music:
> the catch of bridge cables plucked
>> by stone-scented wind; the low, bent
hum of the Delaware, rippling like a singing saw.

There are other cruelties too:
> the extra-inning double in the gap
>> that sends the summer crowd shuffling
for the parking lot. Those are the nights

when any boy would drop
> Pabst empties off the Tacony-Palmyra
>> Bridge, then watch the stars
strip off their summer dresses and dive naked

into the water. I wave from the bridge
> because maybe Lefty's pitching a gem tonight.
>> Maybe the moon's a cut fastball dropping
off the horizon. Maybe 216 strands of loose city light

stitch the sky together. Someone told me
> that the moon was made of cork
>> and leather and old bar songs
and jars of railroad sparks and braided horsehair.

But what's our city made of? Everything's been growing
> too quickly; the skyline's becoming a night
>> brighter than day. Glass-walled buildings
muscle their way up the cityscape, and I've never trusted

anything that doesn't throw a shadow. So come with
       me to the bridge. We'll watch the fireworks
              strain into the night. We can fix their lights
into a constellation of an ox pulling down a house, then let

the spent flakes of soot settle on our eyelids
       like wafers of host dropped onto tongues,
           so that when we open our eyes, we'll
swallow the tiny, failed bodies in every possibility of light.

Vespers

Peel an orange, set
a candle in the rind—

let the smoke melt
the pith into an oil

sweeter than palm.
Before we die,

we taste almonds;
we wake to a lover

slipping a tongue
in our ear;

we confess our sins
in hushed breath

to slats
of grated light.

Dab the oil on the forgotten
parts of yourself:

the eyelid's creases,
the finger's rungs,

the patch of jawbone
hidden by the earlobe.

Saints forget themselves
in their sufferings,

so we recite their names
to remind them

how pain can be pronounced:
oilfield, blood orange, watercress.

Nothing we believe in
mixes: it sifts

the liquor from lime, deposits
drops of sweat

that slide like rosary beads:
a grease that washes everything

clean but us.
Take the candle wax—

spread it on
your lover's lips. Faith

is tasting flesh
through all coverings—

through organ pipe,
through silk,

through our thin skin that keeps
all we are from spilling out.

THE CABINET OF THINGS SWALLOWED

At the medical museum, we fourth-graders crowd around the oddities: the tiny, jarred fetus turning, almost imperceptibly, like the rotation of an infant moon; the model of a syphilitic eye, sagging like the cut fig my father pushed around his plate at breakfast as he read this morning's paper.

Betsy Wilcox follows me from exhibit to exhibit. When she sees the human horn display—a taut, wax face with a stalk like a Black Locust limb sprouting from the forehead—she grabs a fistful of my shirt and buries her face in my chest.

The glass cases of the museum showcase the horror of what our bodies can become. Betsy trails me closely, as we pass the hundreds of fleshy pounds of the world's largest colon, curled and asleep like some biblical slug.

We come to a wooden cabinet with long, thin drawers. The sign reads: "Things Swallowed." I slide out the top drawer to find what I expected: wheat pennies, safety pins, suit buttons, all ranked and filed and labeled with faded script. I close that drawer and open the next. It holds larger treasures: threaded needles, thimbles fuzzed over with rust, fan-shaped seashells, a book of matches from a New York bar.

The items are bigger in each new drawer. The next has a woman's black glove with gold thread tracing the wrist, a light bulb, and a silver pocket watch, still ticking like a tiny robin's heart. The next: a gold collection plate from a Presbyterian church, a red-glazed salt cellar.

I pull open the second-to-last drawer, where there is a single claw hammer. The head is dull black; the handle's wood is wrapped with the stains of fingerprints.

There is one drawer left. "Don't," Betsy says, as I reach for the handle. And in her wide, wet eyes, I can barely see the reflection of the cloud-white marble I swallowed on my fourth birthday.

Dear Doctor Franklin

Everything is an invention,
I've come to learn. The way we press

into each other on the morning train—
that brush of cloth and wool

that seeps into us like a benediction,
or how the old woman

waiting for the bus folds her newspaper
into quarters, and presses it

to her face when she thinks no one
is watching—how the smell of ink

and newsprint reminds her of her
night shifts at the printing plant,

how she crawled into bed
still in boots and a work shirt,

and ran dye-purpled hands
down her neck. I see eyeglasses

on everyone nowadays—
It comforts me to know that light

visits us all differently,
that the imprecisions of our bodies

can work on us the way a cabinetmaker
tends panel after panel

of soft wood. The city rouses slowly
these mornings—I watch it rattle

in the hand-printed windows
of the train. I want to find the line

where the city becomes the city,
where invention becomes instrument.

Some days I see it in the moment
the graffiti thickens near the tunnels,

or when the train stumbles
into the city's shadow—when the light

we know becomes delicate and cruel—
and I see how fragile our eyes will become.

Hard Light Through Hemlock

Damn the snow.
     —Yusef Komunyakaa

My father told me
that all the workings
of our clocks were
turned by tiny ghosts.
I was a child then,
and never knew
the difference
between an eyeful
of snow and an assembly
of spirits manning
the mechanics
of our old house.
I somehow deduced
that every apparition
was made of ice,
so I crossed
myself when the boys
in the schoolyard
ate their handfuls
of playground snow.
Their hot breath
ghosted against the gray
film of January mornings,
and their tongues reddened
as they showed
each other the thin coats
of ice melting
over muscle.
My father's hands

at the piano pushed
against the muscles
of the keys, arranging
each one as if it were
the limb of an artist's
model aching after
a full day's sitting.
Every piano we had
was a kind of ghost—
each one an artifact.
The movers left
the last piano in our yard
while we were away.
We returned to find
an old upright slumped
and half-buried by snow
like a fat doe shot
and forgotten.
Every clock in our house
had unfinished business.
Every note my father
struck in the dark
before he left for work
was another life waiting—
like him—to sleep
through the sunrise.
And every morning
I woke to the clatter
of a hard light
through hemlock,
of a garage door closing,
of a window undoing
the morning, and I could
never help but pull

the covers over my face,
let my breath become
a coat of warmth
that I knew could
never fray.

Ars Poetica

Everything pains to linger
beyond its stay:

the moon begging its way
into the morning sky

like a child
pounding at the embassy gate,

or the breath
against a windowpane

fogging our view of the century oak,
its last leaves traded

for a hundred crows
littering the snow with black tail feathers

and small, clean bones.
When the plowblade finds the body

of an old cello under orchard soil,
the music of iron

cutting wood is too much
for our ears to bear.

If you ask me to linger,
one day I will.

If you ask me to paint
a song inside

a melon, I'll hone
my sharpest knife.

I can't coat trees with grafts
of new branches

if the trees won't ever want for them.
But every day I try—

new limbs turn brittle,
and young buds

rot on the branch. I watch
my stove's belly rust

to cinders while birds
in the cabinetry

build their nest in a copper bowl.
When I can't hear

their song in the veins
of the woodwork, I know

the house will fall,
yet I can't ever help

but stay for far too long.

Dear Doctor Franklin

When we speak, our words do
what we cannot. Every night

I've thought about how long
I can go without putting my lips

to a weathervane, about how
many keys a man can swallow

before never closing his fist again.
There's an argument to how

we caress the joints of a finger,
how we count them like the cool

beads on an abacus. You once wrote
that *God helps those that help themselves.*

I once wrote a letter to a woman
describing how Italian statues

had no toes, because pilgrims
can't keep their hands

from stretching out to touch
something holy, forgetting

that we carry parts of everything
away with us. Tomorrow,

a horse will fall from a bridge
into the river, and a boy

will close his eyes before
it hits the water. He'll tell the story

to his friends the next day.
Like a hand slapping the top

of a piano, is how he'll describe
the sound. I've thought about

what to say in those moments
when there's nothing we can say.

Outside, the trees struggle to shed
their clean skin of ice.

Night settles over us
and the streetlights spread a calendar

of shadows across the sidewalk.
I watch a weathervane spin into the wind.

Like a horse falling from a bridge.
When there's nothing left to say.

CATHEDRALS

We tent our fingers
to make a cathedral.
This is how it's always been
done—how a whisper
between two palms
becomes an architecture
we can't fit into
our mouths. We hear
words like *nave*
and remember shoveling
piles of tulips into
a burnt-out flatbed.
An old man says
cupola, and I think
of knotty loaves
of rye stacked
like cordwood
in the baker's pantry.
I dream of a church's
unfinished dome
squinting upward
like the battered eye-socket
of a bare-knuckle boxer.
Every dream is its own
kind of shaky cathedral—
joists and vaults bracing
it against the weight
of another morning
invoked against us.
There's a cathedral
built from the leg bones
of draft horses and saints.

A cathedral of birds
scaffolding the sky.
A cathedral of bodies
opening to each other
on beds smooth as altars.
A cathedral of hands
unbuttoning the skin
of every prayer
within reach.

Dear Doctor Franklin

All my life I've tried to learn
what digs into our bones,
what uncouples voice

from desire and sets it
out to pasture like the old
piano left in the alley,

now filled with apple skins
and cat shit and wet copies
of the *Daily News*. One day I'll see

how music can play us
through the blues as we walk
under our fat nickel of a moon.

The showmanship of the city
would suit you, I can tell—
the diplomacy of walking

from one neighborhood
to another while drinking
in the liquored music

of each language, smelling
the cantaloupe's sweat
and the strawberry's breath

without remembering how
a coin tastes under the tongue.
I see children leave pennies

on your grave, but I never
have. I know you'd rather
I save mine, claim

the old alley piano
and unveil it in the backyard.
You'd want me to buy

a dog-eared lesson book,
set a thick sandwich on the piano top,
and let each bronzy note bell

its way through the night.
Sometimes I put a penny
on my tongue and think

about blood—how a cut
in the mouth is the only way
we taste mouth; I know

how voice starts from the spine,
how it scales the ribs' fretwork
until it reaches the tongue.

History is all the ways
we fail each other, is not
something you wrote,

but it sounds like it
could be. Give me a pithy saying
to tuck in my pocket.

Give me an almanac
listing all the old places
my father flew his kite.

A Sunday Box

Let the Sabbath be every single thing we take from this chest: let it be the linked rings of wood polished glossier than a calf's eye; let it be the tissue paper folded into thumb-sized mushrooms, delicate enough to wilt in the moment just before they're touched; let it be the velvet compass case, worn so long by age that we couldn't tell it from skin. This chest the size of a mare's chest, this chest of sad-grained wood, this chest locked to every day but the last, was the chest my father's grandfather fashioned in some town or country we long ago forgot. Let the Sabbath be everything in the chest, and everything not in the chest: let it be the thin pistons of starlight turning night's cold engine; let it be the ear of the lamb and the stomach of the lamb and the tongue of the lamb; let it be the train platform like an altar that offers us up each and every evening. When we open the chest, we are the Sabbath and we are of the Sabbath. We are the sea-glass hidden in a fist of seaweed, and we are of the sandpiper's bones worn frail as tinder under salt-rich air. We are the subway stairs grown slick with ice, and we are of the ice that gloves the streetlights. We are of the flesh, but we are not the flesh. Let the Sabbath be the flesh; let the Sabbath be the mouth; let the Sabbath be the hands that build a chest from wet, warped wood—crafted in a country I'll never know, in a town that smells of snow-covered lilac.

Notes on the Twenty-first Century

I wanted so badly for it
to change us, for our muscles
to grow ripe and fat in full view
of those who struggled to forget.
Maybe what we wanted was
to break off a piece of honeycomb
and chew it for an entire afternoon,
to let the wax and honey melt
across our teeth, until the only
remaining answer was a kiss.
I still can't remember the difference
between a paper birch and a white pine
even though I know my father
told me. I left behind so many names
of trees, so many nights rolling
in the pile of dogwood petals
in the backyard. My mother
told me that Christ's cross
was made of dogwood, and never grew
straight again. I can't help
the dogwood any more than the sparrows
that flew into our shutters every summer.
Now, driving through the city, I recite
the names of streets in a prayer
my father taught me: Arch, Race, Vine.
In Fishtown my mother waited
all morning on the stoop of a row house
for the old Ukrainian undertaker—
the only one who could bury
my grandfather. How I wanted
to build a rumor to take it all with me,
to live within the lines of fences

that no longer remember their builders.
How I wanted to make the streets
into the trees they bear the names of—
to walk south of City Hall
through groves of chestnut, walnut, spruce.
To name something is to know it
differently, to call a bridge the Walt Whitman
makes the water long for the land,
and the ferry pilots forget their songs.
That the farmers called this moon
the Worm Moon is something we'll forget—
just as the pavement forgets our footfalls,
the skyline forgets the sunrise,
and the archers forget their bows.

Ode, Elegy, Aubade, Psalm

1

The songbird that escapes
from a burning house
will build its nest
in the shape of a cage.

2

This is one thing
we know: song begs
for the places that make it
grow from seed to starling,

3

places that put the heart's hemlock
in an empty rowboat
and heave it from the shore.

4

We only praise what we cannot
keep: violin strings berried with rain,
teacups overflowing with brandywine,
radios sickened with static.

5

Glass tossed out with the tide
will come back smoother and stranger,
but never to the same person.

6

This is something we want
to know. The woman in love
never touches her ears.

7

The man in his house is always lost
without her.

8

Morning pulls light
from the dark like a boy
hoisting a trout from the lake
by its clean, pink gills.

9

When the woman escapes
from a burning house
she will know the path of the wind,

10

how it writes its scripture
in peach blossoms blown
into a baby's empty pram.

11

She'll feel it compose its words
against her body, against the night,
against the water, in an endless, artless psalm.

STRANGE ELEGY

Some days I wonder
if I could do sleight of hand
if I practiced for days
in front of a mirror.
There are so few ways
to invent objects from air.
To make something
from nothing is a king's craft:
the way my uncle
took his harmonica,
silver as a knife-blade,
and cast his breath
into it until the peeling,
papered walls of my grandfather's
house became a stove
too hot for any boy's hand
to touch. I remember too many things
that I never saw: my grandmother's lips
pressed to a goose egg
and a soft ribbon of yolk
spinning from a pinhole in its shell;
my grandfather's knuckles
big as marbles and his skin
tightening the sicker he grew;
the hot scent of horseradish
steeping through the house
as we ground it fresh
and couldn't stop crying.
If the memories I make are better
than the ones I lose, I'll call
myself a craftsman.
But every night I dream

that our house has died
and my father is alone in the yard,
digging its enormous grave.

Ephesians

Beloved,

Remember what we used to know: the owl perched in the barn rafters with a kitten dangling from its beak, the summers so dry that the wheat withered underfoot as we walked through the field with ice-cream-coated hands. I remember the day you went crazy with fever and took a hatchet to the hives in the apiary. You stood in the swarm and shouted, "I am the Lord God of all creation!" before your father ran in and cradled you to the house. That night, the doctor dipped bandages in honey and wrapped your welted limbs, while your father read to you from Aesop's *Fables*. You opened your mouth and let the doctor reach in with pliers, let him pull one bee after another from under your swollen tongue, and let him hold each corpse—glistened with spit—up to the windowpane, before dropping it in a jar at your bedside. You carried that jar with you always, half-filled with their dried bodies, like kernels of corn. On the last night of summer, we fell asleep in the hayloft. In your dream, you whispered, *wake up, O sleeper, rise from the dead*. In the morning, the jar was empty, and our eyes were the color of nectar.

VIGILS

Here is a morning like a blood-
soaked eye, like an old valve

aching under pressure, like the throat
of a horse marked long with the white

strokes of a surgeon's chalk.
You say to us, *open your eyes—*

We say, *prayer is a wedding
band lost in the onion field.*

We crave the night—its fleet
of stars tacking drunkenly

across the sky, dropping
anchor into the deepening sound

of our open mouths.
The smallest hours are the time

for sacks of oysters hauled
from the cove, for whittling

a cathedral from a cow's horn,
for mapping the forest edge

by dusting off the back-shelf
bottle of bourbon.

I never want to remember
the moment just before sunrise,

when sleeping lovers pull
away from each other,

when libraries re-hide
their secret books,

when the Jesuits finally finish
their evening study.

You say to us, *clasp your hands
and rejoice—the day is newly risen.*

We say, *the most valuable statues
in the world are small enough*

to hide in the mouth. Here
is a Bible hollowed and full

of crickets. Here is a map to
the bones in a child's foot.

Here is a list of theses
written on a woman's stocking.

Before the dawn, we pry open
oysters to drink the meat

and anoint ourselves
with their liquor. Each glassy

mouth of salt never fails to linger,
speaking and shining

on our empty foreheads.

ODE TO A HAWK WITH WINGS BURNING

When our eyes can't adjust
to the fog of late light burning

off under a heat of darkness,
a black flower blooms

for a single minute,
and the bees waiting for its nectar

die of thirst. They drop one by one
into a furry pile around the stem,

not knowing that the scarcity
of its opening fails to make the juice

any sweeter. We lie when we think
that the rare and the sacred

are like twin, unborn colts—legs tangled
as they float in the barrel

of their mother's belly. A girl keeps
a halved pear in a jar by her bedside

and says that it's her dead puppy's ear,
so everyone believes her

when she kisses the glass container
goodnight, and carries it on walks

around the neighborhood. You can learn
the most horrible things, if you listen

in the moment between night and day.
I would name that moment, but to name it

would make it grow, would give old women
the leisure to kneel at the altar and light

candle after candle to ward it all away.
I won't let it have a cadence

of the commonplace. I won't let
my mother's botany book grow any bigger.

I won't let the neighborhood kids catch
another creature from my dreams,

like the day two boys
dipped a hawk in gasoline,

and tossed it into the night
with its wings still burning.

We didn't know what to do when the deer
tangled his antlers in the rusty spokes

of the landfill bicycle at the edge
of town, so we rode

from street to street, leaving
baskets of baby fish

at the doors of every church
we could find. Pray for the filly

with the lame leg. Pray for the father
with the iron burn on his thigh.

Pray for the moon to float down
like a lost paper lantern

that finds a midnight funeral
and settles—still smoldering—

on the bare, burning branches
that cradle the ashes of a hawk.

II.

FOREIGN FILMS

Foreign Film at the Garman Opera House

We can smell the hotel
burning down across the street,

the brine boiling off
barrels of German pickles

in the basement restaurant.
On-screen, we watch a whale

decompose. Two men
pull lengths of skin

from its side, revealing
a red wall of muscle underneath.

They move like old paperhangers,
gently freeing sheets

from the ripe flesh
and setting them in a squared pile.

I like how her glasses reflect
the foggy theater light,

how we pass a small thermos
of wine between us.

In the film, the men rub the whale
with kerosene, and set it alight.

But only half the body burns. Tailbones peek
through the rendering oil like a row

of piano keys dipped in honey. The head drowns
in water. Yet the whale vanishes neatly:

tail and belly eaten by heat that first night,
head cleaned to bone by weeks of salty waves.

By the credits, the smoke seeps
through the door,

and we leave before the music
finishes, into a snow-spotted evening,

where the street corner hotel still burns—
scaffolding silhouetted against flame,

its architecture evolving from form to fume.

THE CITY THAT SWALLOWED THE SEA

I want to forget the city that swallowed the sea,
     where the churches unbreak bread and send old men
onto their hymnaled knees, where the streets sing
     like handbells and the night cracks like a broken bottle
crushed under the heel of a priest taking confessions,
     where the newsmen huddle on a street corner
under evening editions while the rain skins
     their stubbled chins and the creeping asphalt
licks at the face of the shoreline still,
     sipping at the sea, sipping at the salt
that steams up from the waves each sweaty night
     and blankets the shoreline in a tight knit
of creamy silt, and I remember the prayers I said,
     with my knees cupped in sand,
how I prayed to the saints for an intercession,
     how it came like a punch to the blood,
wrapped its fingers around the throat of my blood,
     squeezed the ribs of my blood until I could feel
the nicked edges of broken-blood ribs tickling
     my blood's tiny lungs, those neat, unfurled sails tacking up
and down my veins, and I remember the saint
     of the city, our patron and the patron of bookkeepers,
the patron against lead poisoning, the patron of shims
     and tambourines, the patron of hiccups and tin whistles,
patron of pandemics and against pandemics,
     of ironworkers and against ironworkers, and I want to forget
when I was five, and our teacher told us to draw
     a picture of ourselves, and I drew the skyline above the sea,
said I was changing my name to "The City,"
     and she leaned in close and said that I would never be
the city that swallowed the sea, and my face
     turned warm, and her breath was the dry hush

of the sea as it slides each day from the city,
          and we rope it and haul it back like a brindle calf
with three legs tied, and we drink it a little
          each day, and the censusman knocks every morning
to measure how much we drank,
          and I want to forget our duty to be the city
that swallowed the sea, to be the saints of the city
          that swallowed the sea, and I want to forget those streets
that ribboned and choked and split my bones,
          that sea that skipped down the avenues of my nerves
and planted a kiss on the tiny bronze bell
          that hangs—unpolished—from the stem of my brain.

Foreign Film at the Ritz at the Bourse

The film gives me a fever.
I sweat through the nights,
and my sister slices an avocado

into cool, fatty strips
she lays across my forehead.
I dream scenes from the film:

a schoolgirl suckling handfuls
of dirt from her closed fist;
a medical student stitching

together half a pig's heart
and half a pomegranate.
My sister takes steeped tea

leaves and spreads them
on my chest. A reporter writes
a novel that no one reads,

and—in the film—is thrown in jail.
A woman copies the psalms
across her belly. Two men fight

over the last copy of the newspaper.
I'm put in a tub full of ice.
My sister pours cupfuls of salt

over me and washes my legs
with her cold hands. The medical student
hides the novel in a cadaver's chest.

My sister puts the radio on low.
She balances a cutting board on the sink
and practices segmenting an orange.

The front page of the morning paper
has a spot of blood under the date.
A spider dangles under the faucet.

At the end of the film, a smuggler
opens a body looking for a book,
but instead finds a tiny metropolis,

a model by an architect of no fame
or import, built of some city
that not even I can recognize.

III.

METROPOLITAN SUITE

Sing! the men chant from the square. A woman sits on the statue of Lenin and strums a silver mandolin. There is center; there is periphery; there is a carousel spinning in the river like a miller's wheel. People from across the world came to reclaim their losses from the museum, and then they decided to stay. If ever you need an umbrella, just go to the lost and found and say, I lost my black umbrella. When they ask, *Is this the one?* answer, *Yes! Thank God you found it, my treasure, my prize, my jewel of the Americas.* This is the City of the Big Shoulders. This is Brotherly Love. These are Angels salt-packed in tin. The woman on the statue sings for days—*city, my love.* We hear it and it is true.

We eat lunch in Jaffa, where the streets are the color of dust shaken from a sparrow's wing. I hold an orange in my hand and listen to the call to prayer falling from the minaret. Cucumbers sliced thin on bone-glassy china. Fish on ice in Reading Terminal stacked like shiny railroad ties. In my hand, the orange peels—a little at first, rind skinning itself from muscle-colored segments of flesh. In the history books, a child dies at every turn in the Tiber. The museum and its wall of eyes. The salt air settling in the veins of the orange. Whittling through us like a prayer.

When they buried the general's heart with his mother's body in Rasos Cemetery, all the oak leaves turned the color of bone. The students washed their feet in the Neris River, and marched on Vingis Park. They clenched their fists so tightly that the police thought they were holding nautilus shells. At the river's rise, the Neris is the Vilija, Byzantium is Istanbul, and New Orleans is still New Orleans. When crab, eels, flounder, and shrimp shipwreck themselves on the shore overnight, the townsfolk call it a jubilee. When they find a teapot-sized heart among the claws and kelp, only the dogs take notice.

When she left, she left her stockings everywhere. Slung over the banister, draped atop the kitchen chairs, wrapped around the handle of the fridge. She left them balled in front of the *Mona Lisa* at the Louvre, left them as bookmarks in the poetry at Shakespeare and Company, left them dangling and wind-blown from the bridges over the Seine. I found them in the elevator of the Empire State Building, in the mailbox outside the Navy Building, nestled in the tree branches at Penn's Landing. My friends said they saw a pile of them on the Metro as they were heading to the Latin Quarter. Stray dogs that wander under the Eiffel Tower at night attack them, mistaking their crumpled form for those of rats. My friends ask if I'm sure they all belong to her. I know, I tell them. No silk that touches her skin has ever felt the same.

City of churches, city of cathedrals. Scooters buzz through the streets like a swarm of shiny beetles, and the statues' marble is soft as flesh. Forgive the coppery taste of a beer made in Pottsville. Forgive the water from the fountain on Capitoline Hill. The seven hills, the seven sisters, the streets named after enough trees to make an orchard at the edge of San Francisco. I could touch the *Pietà*, if I wanted. I could touch Monet's *Water Lilies*. I could touch the Liberty Bell and go to jail for a year and a day. The women here walk down the street as if they're modeling for Botticelli. The men drink their beer in the piazzas, and sip liquor strong enough to peel the skin from a plum.

It's a mistake to think the city can be divided, can be parsed or parceled, trimmed or truncated. In erasing what we wanted to forget, we learned to remember through absence. The bombs make and unmake in equal measure. We broke down a wall and took it away, then broke down its image and took that away too. The silt in the Mississippi feels like threads of cotton sliding between fingers. The water is fast and warm, but the city doesn't remember what it's like to build bridges without steel, or burn paper houses for week after week. From the Walt Whitman Bridge, we can see the stadiums bloated like kettle drums. We can see the city working hard to forget.

I read a story about revolutionaries catching black dogs and hanging their dead bodies from light posts. When they ran out of black dogs, they started painting any dead dog black, splattering their rhetoric across the city, across the body of anything with enough muscle to support its own skin. But this was just a story I read, a fiction that even said as much. I read another story about an immigrant in Chicago who began to vanish. And another about a man who returns to Philadelphia and finds they burned part of it down. Last night, I read a story about a man who can't build a fire and dies in the cold: the city that stills us all, with its slow-moving trains and its arctic-brilliant nights.

Sunday morning in Jackson Heights, the street vendors cook their tamales—the ripe, green smell of peppers roasting black on burners, the subway station rattling overhead like a misshapen music box. On Market, the Chinese food cart sells fresh cuttlefish; men and women wedge their briefcases under their arms and hold their orders with both hands, letting the tentacles dangle loosely over the plate's edge. Outside the Tube, a man sells sweet, greasy kebabs wrapped in wax paper—the shiny, black cabs stop in front of him, and he shoves an order through each window, collecting a wad of pounds before the drivers speed away. At the Met, I walk through the long, white arcade of Greek sculptures—missing arms, missing legs, missing heads—and almost hear the hum of mopeds all around me, the song of students chanting in the streets.

The boats haul snow into the Baltic as ballast, and return to port stuffed with sardines. At the cocktail party, each cube of ice has a hummingbird heart frozen in its center. When the vodka wears away the ice, one last bloom of red pumps into the liquor. Wind papers the windows of the Metro with cherry blossoms, and in Red Square rail workers pin roses in their caps. Red is the copper we strip from row houses; red is the body that eats the body; red is the summer stink our dogs hide under the house from.

In Simón Bolívar Park, the kites cut the sky into cities: city of red kites, city of square kites, city of sad kites struggling to stay aloft. The children eat soft pretzels doused with mustard and fat sausages piled high with peppers. They rub the feet of the Rodin statues outside the museum. They yell, *My city!*, *my city!* and point to sections of the sky. I tell them that there's only one sky and they must share it all—it can't be portioned or purposed. *Does that mean there's only one city, too?* they ask me. I don't know what to tell them, because I know they want the truth.

In the shade of the Admiralty Building, a girl peels frost from the petals of a buttercup. The Winter Palace squatly waits in the square, like a caviar-laden boxcar halted by spring snow. Cold finds the slivers of body we show to the world; it makes a woman tug at her glove with her teeth as she cradles her baby against her. She watches the Admiralty's weathervane—a small, gold ship—scatter slim coins of morning light along the sidewalk as the wind picks up. Her baby reaches out for the light, his tiny hands clasping the air, his tiny teeth growing cold from laughter.

Tell me about the law, she says. The gaslights burn dimly in the morning light, like the sleepy eyes of too-long-awake children. I tell her the law is like a bull with a cracked horn nosing up to a barbed-wire fence. I look at her pendant, set against the soft plate of skin where her neck meets her chest. Some cities have too many statues, I say, some have too few. The statue in front of the Teatro Colón wasn't artistic enough, so the mayor had it moved. She tells me she loves bridges—how the stitches of them hold the city together; every river is a seam on a dress, but they're always ready to burst. She mouths to me the word *Monongahela*. The gaslights run all day. The city is so full of law that it's tearing itself apart.

The city takes the Atlantic and makes it into more city. The district was water; now an echo of ocean caresses the skin-slick streets. We count people like grains of rice, like palm seeds, like islands in an archipelago. The stars smell of gasoline and rusty shears, while the harvest-heavy wheat lays itself down like an orphaned lamb. In London, the streets smell of picture frames and owl feathers; in Haifa they smell of crushed oranges and salted almonds. The night after two buses crashed, I picked through the wreckage and found yams, plantains, and a basket of chilies so red that I thought they had been stained with blood.

City of anvils. City of rotten figs. City whose ground shakes like a bedsheet on the laundry line. City of heartflies. City like a doe's tail snagged by thistle. City of forts in the woods. Our city of dictionaries. Our city of prayers in bottles. Thin-wristed city. Alibi city. City of the gospel of empty ballot boxes. Stained glass city. Rose-quartz city. City of coin collectors and unkempt legislators. City of endless airplay. City I track by its limping gait. City like a harp's dusty strings. City like an unbuckled belt. Frontier city. Port city. Parable city. City where we gathered under summer's shade of flies. City where every bell we rang couldn't help but break.

CIRCLES

Let what begins
continue. Let
your dog turn

up his nose at
the plate of vegetables
you delicately

smashed on the floor.
How far are we now
from the place

they sealed the boy
inside the well
when they couldn't

figure out how
to save him?
They didn't want to

hear his cries anymore.
So they boarded up
the mouth and continued

with the picnic,
even as their children
grew wet with rain.

This summer,
tornadoes will
circle our town,

a runaway will
circle her final
destination on a map,

and dogs will
stalk circles around
a wounded deer.

I couldn't tell
you how to dress
that leg. You've never

been alone before,
but I forget that
sometimes. I know

how to make bandages
from bedsheets;
my grandmother told me

stories from the war,
how her garden was
full of scrap metal,

how she served tomatoes
dressed in oil and rust,
yet sweeter than before.

She'd say, *let what begins
continue*, and gesture
vaguely at the sky,

as if the sky was where
everything happened.

NOTES

"The Cabinet of Things Swallowed" is based on an exhibit at the Mütter Museum in Philadelphia.

The "Dear Doctor Franklin" poems are inspired by Wayne Miller's "Dear Sappho," poems.

The epigraph and title of "Hard Light Through Hemlock" come from Yusef Komunyakaa's poem "Elegy for Thelonious."

Acknowledgments

Many thanks to the editors of the following journals where these poems appeared, sometimes in earlier forms:

Copper Nickel: "Notes on the Twenty-first Century";
Crab Orchard Review: "Vespers," "Vigils";
DIAGRAM: "Ode, Elegy, Aubade, Psalm";
Mid-American Review: "The Cabinet of Things Swallowed";
Ninth Letter: "Circles";
The Pinch: "Ephesians";
Pleiades: "The City That Swallowed the Sea";
Puerto del Sol: "Philadelphia, 1976";
Redivider: "Foreign Film at the Garman Opera House";
The Southern Review: Selections from "Metropolitan Suite";
Sycamore Review: "Ode to a Hawk with Wings Burning";
Third Coast: "Foreign Film at the Ritz at the Bourse";
Waccamaw: "Hard Light Through Hemlock," the first "Dear Doctor
    Franklin";
Washington Square: "Strange Elegy";
West Branch Wired: Selections from "Metropolitan Suite".

"The Cabinet of Things Swallowed" was chosen by Aimee Nezhukumatathil as the winner of *Mid-American Review*'s Fineline Competition.

"Philadelphia, 1976" was chosen by Oliver de la Paz for an AWP Intro Journals Award.

Many thanks to Jane Hirshfield for choosing this book for the A. Poulin Jr. Prize and for her invaluable editorial insights.

Thanks to Peter Conners and the staff at BOA Editions for their peerless dedication and editorial expertise.

I owe a great debt to all my teachers, especially Cathy Bowman, Maurice Manning, Scott Russell Sanders, and Maura Stanton. Their generous teaching helped me beyond measure. And special thanks to all my friends and colleagues at Indiana University.

Thanks to Stanford University for their generous gift of a Wallace Stegner Fellowship, which allowed me to complete this book.

Thanks to Kelly Wilson.

Thanks to Marcus Wicker.

Endless thanks to Ross Gay—my teacher, friend, and mentor.

And above all, thank you to my parents. This book is for them.

About the Author

Ryan Teitman is a Wallace Stegner Fellow in poetry at Stanford University. He received his BA in English at Penn State, worked as a newspaper reporter in and around Philadelphia, and earned an MFA in Creative Writing and an MA in English from Indiana University. His poems have appeared in *Crab Orchard Review*, *Pleiades*, *Sycamore Review*, *Third Coast*, and other journals, and his work has received an AWP Intro Journals Award and several Pushcart Prize nominations. He currently lives in Berkeley, California.

BOA Editions, Ltd.
The A. Poulin, Jr. New Poets of America Series

Colophon

Litany for the City, poems by Ryan Teitman, is set in Bernhard Modern, a digital version of the font designed by the graphic artist Lucian Bernhard (1883–1972) and first cut by American Type Founders in 1937.

The publication of this book is made possible, in part, by the special support of the following individuals:

Anonymous

Anne Germanacos

Suzanne Gouvernet

Robin, Hollon & Casey Hursh, *in memory of Peter Hursh*

X. J. & Dorothy M. Kennedy

Keetje Kuipers, *in memory of Maximillian Veracity Kane*

Jack & Gail Langerak

Katherine Lederer

Boo Poulin

Deborah Ronnen & Sherm Levey

Steven O. Russell & Phyllis Rifkin Russell

Ellen & David Wallack

Glenn & Helen William

❖